This book belongs to:
www.cowboydogseries.com

Mud Boots

Written by Mary Stern Illustrated by Anna-Maria Crum

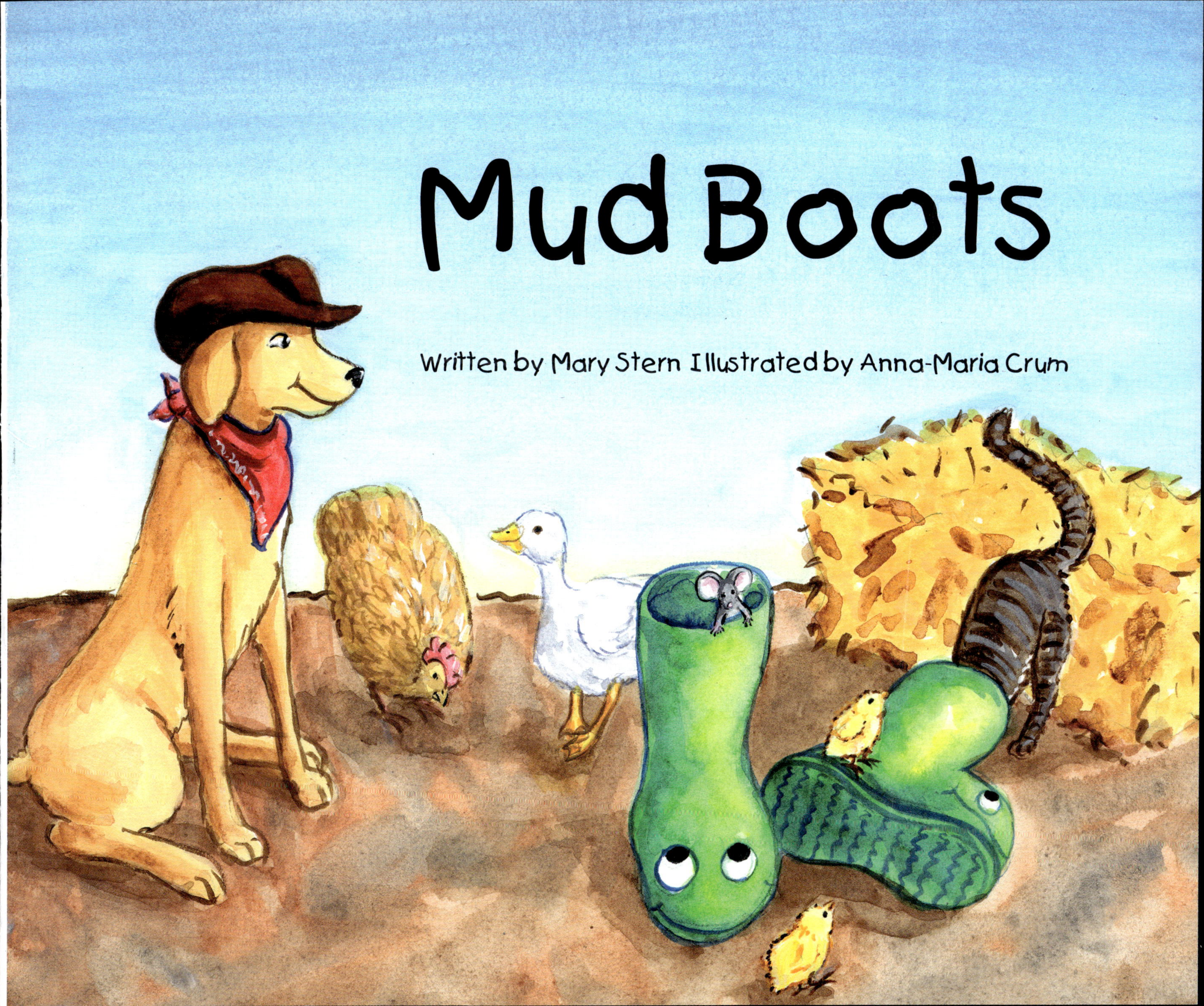

To my mother who read to me and gave me a love of reading and books.

Eileen Ramsey
1915-2009

To the farmers of the United States who feed the world especially to my farm friends, the Hageman family and the Gearhart family.

Part of the proceeds from the sale of this book will be donated to MMRF in memory of Bob Debaun.

Text by Mary Stern
Illustrations and book design by Anna-Maria Crum

CURRENT PRINTING
10 9 8 7 6 5 4 3 2 1

Library of Congress Cataloging – in Publication Data
Stern, Mary
Mud Boots by Mary Stern; illustrations by Anna-Maria Crum. 32 p. cm.
Summary: Grandma, Brandon and Tawny take a tour of the farm.
ISBN: 978-0-9801602-2-2
1. Nature – Juvenile Literature. I. Stern, Mary. II. Title.

The illustrations for this book were done in acrylics on illustration board.

The title of the book "Mud Boots" was submitted by Sara Porter.

Printed and bound in USA.

For information, contact Mary Stern at www.cowboydogseries.com.

Grandma,
I'll put on my mud boots so we can go out.
We'll see lots of things as we wander about.

You can walk, but I get to ride.
Cowboy Dog can sit by my side.

Look at the vegetables in our garden plot.
Some are ripe and some are not.

There are root vegetables like beets and potatoes.
And some grow on vines like peas and tomatoes.

The farmers say "Knee high by the 4th of July."
By August the corn will be ready to try.

Look out in the field. That's our new billy.
He's prancing around and acting quite silly.

Step into the barn. There's lots to see.
But things may be hiding from you and me.

Look up and down and all around
Above the hayloft and on the ground.

Up in the rafters swallows glide.
And under the tractor mice can hide.

The barn cat sits on a bale of hay.
He's hoping the mice will come his way.

You may think the hen is taking a rest.
But she's sitting on eggs she laid in her nest.

The ducks and geese are free to roam.
But in the evening they will come home.

Let's go to the pasture. The horses are there.
There's a young pony and a beautiful mare.

The miniature donkey is standing nearby.
He can be stubborn. He can be shy.

Brandon

Brandon is a five year old farm boy.
He loves his farm, animals, garden and riding on his John Deere tractor.
He lives with his parents, two brothers, horse, pony, miniature donkey, six goats, ducks, chickens, cats and dogs on a farm in Kansas.

photo by Leah Mick Images.

Tawny

Tawny is an eight year old Mountain View Cur.
She lives in Santa Barbara and can be seen at Douglas Preserve "doggie" park.

There's so much to see and so much to do.
I love sharing my farm with you.